MW01110101

HOOK

Peter LaBerge

SIBLING RIVALRY PRESS
LITTLE ROCK, ARKANSAS

WWW.SIBLINGRIVALRYPRESS.COM

Hook
Copyright © 2015 by Peter LaBerge

Cover art by Brian Oldham

Author photo by William Sulit
Cover design by Seth Pennington

Sibling Rivalry Press, LLC
PO Box 26147
Little Rock, AR 72221

info@siblingrivalrypress.com

www.siblingrivalrypress.com

ISBN: 978-1-937420-97-0

First Sibling Rivalry Press Edition, October 2015

CONTENTS

COMPOSITION

I found the forest where I was allowed to hate
and I built my body inside it.

Evangelists say there were times like this.

*

Around the nearest town, I distribute
fliers saying things like this could matter one day.

They listen, the wood knots of my mind.

*

I call the body what it wills to be—a sack
of feathers, a shot of gin—

a sack of feathers, a mile of flight.

GLADIOLUS

Children have chained their families
     with the stalks, learned departures
as mother-petals, father-scents.

Children have caught the newest
     blossoms between their fingers—
petals scattered, fathers smelling the centers

of their wives. Mothers tell their children
     that God sleeps in the faded
mouths of simple creatures. Children,

quiet as cream, praying
     to feel the bones of another
animal in their teeth.

FIELD SERMON: ON ABSTINENCE

The boy doesn't care

about Portland anymore.

About what Elvis would say

to that. *Today is all about*

the bees. It hasn't been this way

since his lips met a bee

in a beer can the summer

before seventh grade. He believes

Jesus made him, hopes

he will be stung in the mirror.

BAISLEY POND, 1989

Father the miracle. Father the present
disciple. Father who kneeled at the edge

of every pond before testing his step.
My vocation was of dare, to be inside

the pond I broke through that winter.
My hands drenched and blue as Gulliver

trout. What I could feel grasping at strands
of him as I found them. River furrows

sheathing what he'd never seen, the season
still too early. We could never tell

which surfaces were safest to touch, which might
fill our boots with a thrill so numbing

we could never unlearn it.

RODEO

First, the bedsheets
unlearn the language

of each body I've ever
loved. The bed bucks

shadows like rodeo
clowns, lungs stable

in their nest of cordwood
until the wind blows

the whole house down.
The panels of sun softer

than silk. *It does not come
quickly*, mothers say, *learning*

to unravel someone else. I unzip
the dress with a god's intimacy—

first the shoulders, then
the spine. Pin and wheel.

APRICOTS

       Today we picked apricots
from the grassy elbows

of your parents' field
           far enough away

    they couldn't
see us stealing the crop

    from the kitchen window
& we ate and we smashed

& we used seeds to spell out
           childhood crushes

    inside the steel-toothed
mouths of barns

   at night a wide-eyed
county lot of them

       hollering
orange into every listening

window
   I tapped against

every unhooked
     window jaw

  I felt a dimming
stroke of rind

      branded
       & made

no match for this
     wandering press

the hand
   christened by mine

       his fingers
         so meaningful

his fingers
  so wide

DESIRES

Hunger is near the end
of our biology textbook, waiting

for something. Your body is a mirror
and in it I can see mine open, broken.

We flip to the page with the organs,
salmon-colored and empty, waiting

for something. *This*, you tell me,
is where hunger is located. Now I go

into the bedroom. Another
mirror waits in the bathroom.

Dependable. An inky heart-shaped
muscle against the cold musket

of my forearm, my shoulder
a barrel singing *cease, fire, cease.*

HARVEST ELEGY

We learn it starts in one line and continues
to the next. Mothers warm

rosary beads in their palms, learn
what their sons do to men

inside their heads. Desire devout and purple.
Fathers say sell it with the plums, pretend

the world hasn't created this. We know
we can only jar this fruit, never grow another.

*

We bite into the world and watch
a man enter the barn's waiting mouth.

We listen to the farmhand's song and watch
the wind drown it in the slop bed.

We listen to the farmhand's song and feel
his cheeks flushed as the barn's face.

We finger pocketed notes and learn
how gentle fathers respect their sons.

We finger pocketed nickels and feel
something inside of our chests bristle.

We bite into the world and taste
the men kissing behind the bales of hay.

STAINED GLASS

Pick up your pieces. Your body—
shards lining the pew rows, the still-

glittering sills. Bring yourself
back before dark. The body lasts

for only the burn of this candle.
The baptism of the eyes, the vacant

dais. Cite the apology of John and his
raindrop, the passage with no flame

lasting more than a mile. Pick up
your pieces. Paint the advent cross

suspended in your mind, a fresh indigo
called *starless night* staining the floor.

FIELD SERMON: SEAGLASS

Speak the language of broken
harmonicas: of things sharp

and unfinished, Billy Joel bent
at the waist, the minor chord

when all the jukeboxes of Miami
have run their battles, digested

their nickels, or maybe when
there is no money at all.

                    *

On being part of yourself:
punching your breasts

to flatten these edges.
Quick moments.

ELPENOR

FOR MATTHEW SHEPARD

I.

When Pound describes it, he seems careless
as an advent candle under the flamed weight

of other boys. One knocks him with his
father's hunting rifle. He slides from light—

wax into a trivet. Acres away, his brothers
spoon brackish water into dry mouths

to understand how it feels to be neither something
nor something else. With stretched sail, their boat

chews on the bitter sea until daybreak. Down
the road, two boys drive him to a field, split

his skin until they've reached the water
beneath it. Slowly, everything of him flows

into boots, stains their socks with cold. No longer
Elpenor, nor Tiresias, nor Matthew, but merely

under the weight of himself: a close-
webbed sea of mist, something people could

write about but never feel again.

II.

Life feels malleable as blown glass,
fragile as an advent candle

in a house with no windows.
From outside the ocean catches

every sinner, reduces them to sand
whistle and whale bone. The boat

sits graveside—vacant and bored
as a pearl. Is there enough

space in what remains of this poem
to name him Christ? *Heap up mine*

arms, be tomb by sea-bord, and inscribed:
The savior falls against himself

like a music note. Now only
the wind can touch him.

III.

Two boys tore a moment
from itself like life

from bone. Mid-October
moths banged against the wind

in sympathy. The night slipped
on itself, more taken with traces

of blood on its hands. After God
laid a frock across the woodpile,

the wind tore it away. For every
afterlife he earned, the boy of ill star

waded through marshland, glimpsed
his brothers riding golden braids.

MASTER THE TEMPEST IS RAGING

If God sends me a wind
    tonight, I might capsize

        into His lap. His fingers
    over me, still the trace of salt.

If we were the boat, I would be
    the sea for Him, pride

in such idleness. Stowed
    within the hull, a school

        of unlucky trout: so poor
    and flopping, they must have

more to say. I am sure
    a man on another coast

        has capsized but tonight
    this is my wish. From him,

I'd hear the summoning
    of a better world and find

all the right winds.

HOOK

It was the summer I learned the difference
between muscle and mussel, my father

and the boy he found washed-up and empty-
mouthed the last night of the fishing trip.

Proud of how I chose wine over seawater
three nights in a row. My fingers spun fast

around the skirted spool, brought him
gasping through the reeds. I whispered his name

until it spread a thin current over us, dragged
something away I could never replace.

I passed a note to him like a fish baited
on a rod, wriggling from a son to his proud

father. The sand strewn with more
mussel carcasses. The shells blackened, vacant

as memory in my father's calloused hands.

FIELD SERMON: WALNUT CREEK

Quiet, the toaster. Quiet, the scalloped

flesh. Saints wander the boy's head

like men lost in hallways, like children

watching mothers mop mornings

into nightgowns spread wide across

concrete floors. Scarecrows in the shed

long-bleached and convinced they are still

the men they pretended to be. The boy

pieces together remnants of the broken

weathervane, foreclosed farm. His body

white as a fox underbelly, a consolation or prayer.

SILO

Inside the silo, I undressed
another man's mouth.

I kissed until I knew his name
and the wind blew east for morning.

*

The world invited rainwater
between the bicycle tracks.

The world invited rainwater
between the lips of its wound.

*

I erased my past fallen
clean from the sky.

So easy for the beauty
to un-exist.

*

I kissed until my tongue
set into the trees.

MISSIONARY

The man claimed the forest
of me. He knew the snow

had chewed the road
to bits, led me blushing

through the melt. The wilt
of the crocuses made

beautiful inside my palm.
Mid-winter. The snow

so heavy, field too purple
to trust. I learned the etiquette

of him, forgot about the bloom
until I saw it on my face.

PHOTO

When I listen, I can hear
    what's left of this forest.

    This plank, this body I once wanted
to lakebottom. In the dark months

    I owned this barren nape of neck.

*

    I imagine glory as ending
        the winter of this world

with a single match. How righteous
    to make the body work

    what it loves.

*

Snow falls, and snow
    rises and what is white

        is good as lost. Beneath the ice
the world preserves its dark. Do not be

fooled—the coal burning through
    the snow is not the snow.

FIELD SERMON: CORONET

Beside the cupboard
where he bakes

light in Betty Crocker
cake-pans, the boy

wants to experience
dawn, every word

the neighbor's radio
has to say. He wishes

he had worn an apron
today, watches words

sizzle and spit, bubble
up, become memory.

The kitchen window
consumes the dew's

promise: *I will meet
your body without chill.*

Yet each time he trusts
his body is torn

into fingertip mist.

THE LAKE

is filled with men. Still the rocks
bed together in the spindle

of the dark, still the lake's cold
swims through my ear.

In the backstroke of the night
I hear the song of the lakeswept—

by entering my body, it turns
to sediment. I am still so cold

to this morning's touch but could
never be dead. In fact I grow

each time a man steals his shadow
from the river, and the river echoes

like the emptying jar it is.

CALL TO WORSHIP

This winter I am breaking

                  every rule of winter. I wash
my body with scented soap. I dig

to find the boy

                  I met twice
behind the bales of wheat.

Now that I have

                  I start to refill this plot
of earth, but no matter how much

I shovel, these moments buckle

                  the ground, knot the frost: *Once, I let
my face down into his river. Once*

I filled his body with stones.

PETER

I have named you Peter because he was the first
apostle to learn the journey, to chart

each hill of me.

*

Night stains the bookshelves. The moon,
white and swallowed.

A floor buckling to the ceiling, my throat.
The moon from you to my mouth.

*

My shoulders melting,
wickless, into this dish of skin.

My shoulders gleaming
through a slit as wide as a post slot.

*

I don't know how to say I've never tasted
the inside of someone else.

I don't know how to say our blessed name.

HOOK

ACKNOWLEDGMENTS

Gracious acknowledgment to the editors of the following publications, which first published or recognized the following poems, often in younger forms:

Best New Poets 2014: "Peter"

Copper Nickel: "Harvest Elegy" and "Call to Worship"

Diagram: "Composition," "Photo," and "Field Sermon: Seaglass"

DIALOGIST: "Baisley Pond, 1989"

Hobart: "Field Sermon: Coronet" and "Field Sermon: On Abstinence"

Indiana Review: "Silo"

Ninth Letter Online: "Rodeo" and "The Lake"

Polyphony H.S.: "Stained Glass"

Out of Sequence: The Sonnets Remixed: "Field Sermon: Walnut Creek"

Redivider: "Elpenor [I]"

Thrush Poetry Journal: "Elpenor [II]"

Vinyl Poetry: "Gladiolus"

Weave Magazine: "Desires"

Word Riot: "Hook" and "Master the Tempest Is Raging"

Thank you to the following institutions who have recognized work from this manuscript: The Alliance for Young Artists & Writers, Hollins University, the Bucknell University Stadler Center for Poetry, the University of Pennsylvania, the Poetry Society of Virginia, and the Poetry Society of the United Kingdom.

Putting this book together would not have been possible without insight, support, friendship, and inspiration from the following individuals: Bryan Borland & Seth Pennington, D. Gilson, Timothy Liu, Talin Tahajian, Richie Hofmann, Wendy Barker, Claudia Cortese, Dorianne Laux, Eduardo C. Corral, Chloe Honum, Joshua Rivkin, Margaret Funkhauser, Ocean Vuong, Brandon Courtney, Douglas Ray, Alexa Derman, Oriana Tang, Maddie Kim, Yasmin Belkhyr, Amanda Silberling, Alina Grabowski, and my parents, Deborah & Jon LaBerge. Further thanks to the Greens Farms Academy English Department (especially Elizabeth F. Cleary) and to the University of Pennsylvania Department of Creative Writing (especially Al Filreis, Jamie-Lee Josselyn, Michelle Taransky, and Gregory Djanikian).

Finally, thank you to Matthew Shepard, Bobby Griffith, and their brave families. Thank you, thank you, thank you.

ABOUT THE POET

Peter LaBerge was born in Connecticut. His poems appear in *Beloit Poetry Journal, Redivider, The Journal, Sixth Finch, Best New Poets 2014, Hayden's Ferry Review*, and *Indiana Review*, as a finalist for the 2015 *Indiana Review* Poetry Prize. The recipient of a fellowship from the Bucknell University Stadler Center for Poetry, he is the co-editor of *Poets on Growth* (Math Paper Press, 2015), the Founder & Editor-in-Chief of *The Adroit Journal*, and an undergraduate student at the University of Pennsylvania.

ABOUT THE ARTIST

Brian Oldham is a fine art photographer and visual artist from Southern California. He is currently living and working near the Los Angeles area and is available for commissioned work internationally. [brianoldham.format.com]

ABOUT THE PRESS

Sibling Rivalry Press is an independent press based in Little Rock, Arkansas. Its mission is to publish work that disturbs and enraptures. This book was published in part due to the support of the Sibling Rivalry Press Foundation, a non-profit private foundation dedicated to assisting small presses and small press authors.

CPSIA information can be obtained
at www.ICGtesting.com
Printed in the USA
BVOW08s0522290417
482536BV00010B/546/P

9 781937 420970